The Ten Commandments of Getting Hired

By: **DAVID HOTTLE, CPC, BILL LINS, CPC**

Copyright 2010

All rights reserved. This book, or parts thereof, may not be reproduced in any form without permission from the author.

CONTENTS

Introduction   6

Commandment One: Thou Shalt Have a Direction Before Starting Your Search   9

    What Field Should I Choose?   10

    How To Evaluate Your Results   12

    CLAMPS   13

    Mentors   15

    Clean Up Your Online Profile   17

    Are You Ready For Commandment Two   19

COMMANDMENT TWO: Thou Shalt Craft The Tools Needed To Search   20

    What Is a Resume   21

    Different Types Of Resumes   23

    Summary-Objective   24

    Accomplishments   25

    Employment History   26

    Education   27

    Activities And Groups   29

    Cover Letters   31

    Professional References   32

    Are You Ready For Commandment Three   34

COMMANDMENT THREE: Thou Shalt Walk Softly Among The Advertised Openings 36

A x E x E = R 37
Advertised Openings 38
Job Boards 39
Establishing A Bulls Eye Employer List 41
Company Websites 42
Resume Metrics 44
Are You Ready For Commandment Four 45

COMMANDMENT FOUR: Thou Shalt Be Proactive Versus Reactive 46

Inbound Vs Outbound Calls 47
Your Telephone Voice 48
Inbound Calls From Potential Employers 49
Outbound Calls To An Employer Following Up On A Job Posting 50
Outbound Calls To An Employer Following Up After An Application 51
Talking To A Live Human Resource Person 52
Voice Mail To Human Resources 53
Making Job Fairs Work For You 54
Are You Ready For Commandment Five 57

COMMANDMENT FIVE: Thou Shalt Covet Your Neighbors Connections 59

What Is Networking And Why Is It Important To Finding A Job? 60
Networking Groups 61

How To Stand Out From The Crowd	62
How To Explain What You Do In a Unique Way	63
Mastering The Coffee Connection	64
Got Goals	65
Are You Ready For Commandment Six?	66
COMMANDMENT SIX: Honor But Use Social Networking Information To Your Advantage	67
What Is Social Networking	68
Why Social Networking Is Important In Securing a Job	69
How To Use Social Networking To Secure Interviews	70
Using Social Networking To Obtain Information That Can Be Used In An Interview	72
How Many Contacts Are Needed	73
Are You Ready For Commandment Seven?	74
COMMANDMENT SEVEN: Thou Shalt Be Prepared For The Path Ahead	76
Your 30 Second Elevator Pitch	77
Feature Benefit	79
Know Your Interviewer	81
Five Frequently Asked Questions By An Employer	82
Top 5 Questions t Ask In An Interview	85
Top 5 Questions To NOT Ask In An Interview	87
Positive Spin On A Negative Past	89
Are You Ready For Commandment Eight?	91
COMMANDMENT EIGHT: Thou Shalt Interview To Get The Job Offer	93

Applicant Be Aware	94
The Purpose Of An Interview	95
Rapport Building In The Interview	96
Interview Preparation	98
Prepping For a Structured Behavioral Interview	99
Sample Behavioral Interview Questions	102
A Telephone Interview	106
Filling Out The Job Application	108
The Face To Face Interview	110
Closing Out The Interview	115
Are You Ready For Commandment Nine?	117
COMMANDMENT NINE: Thou Shalt Follow Up For Success	119
The Keys To Interview Follow Up	120
Making A Thank You Call	122
The Thank You Note or Email	124
A Second Interview	125
Prepping For A Second And Subsequent Interviews	126
Post Interview Follow Up	127
Are You Ready For Commandment Ten?	128
COMMANDMENT TEN: Thou Shalt Get a Job Offer	130
What Is A Bonafide Job Offer	131
Don't Say No Immediately To a Job Offer You Do Not Like	133
How Do I Enhance My Job Offer	135
Accepting A Job Offer And Before You Start	136

INTRODUCTION

Let us begin your career transition journey with a little story.

A farmer went out to sow his seed.
As he was scattering the seed, some fell along the path;
It was trampled on and the birds of the air ate it up.
Some fell on rock, and when it came up, the plants withered because they had no moisture.
Other seed fell among thorns, which grew up with it and choked the plants.
Still, other seed fell on good soil. It came up and yielded a crop a hundred times more than was sown.

How does this little story relate to your job search?

The Answer:

The seed is the information contained in books like this and other material that shares "How To" knowledge.

Those along the path are the ones who have been taught the "How To's" but all along believed they could do it better. So they do not include the information from their daily job search routine so that they may not believe in it and prosper.

Those on the rock are the ones who receive the "How To" information during their job search and understand it is successful. But they have no root. They believe it for awhile, but when the search takes a little longer or when things get a little tough, they lose confidence.

The seed that fell among the thorns stands for those who learn the "How To" information, but as they go on their way they are choked full by life's worries, outside influences, negative feedback and let their personal problems interfere, and they fail because of it.

But the seed on good soil stands for those with the proper attitude, motivations and work ethics, who learn the "How To" information, retain it, use it every day of their job search, and by persevering get hired in the job they want.

Which will you be; the path, the rock or the good soil?

COMMANDMENT ONE

Thou Shalt Have a Direction Before Starting Your Search

"Without counsel, plans go wrong, but with many advisers they succeed."

Prov. 15:22

What Field to Choose?

You're probably already aware that there are many factors and opinions regarding what sort of career you should build for yourself.

So, what's your first step? Well, that begins with this fundamental challenge: What Profession is for you?

You probably find yourself asking, *"Where do I start? Where do I go from here?"*

Taking Career Assessment tests are a good start. There are many assessment tests out there, even some that are free. Simply do an internet search for "Free Career Assessment Tests" or "Career Assessment Tests" and you should find what you need.

Next, you must identify and truly lean on mentors ... people who can guide you and give you honest, constructive feedback because they were once where you are today and have successfully journeyed down their chosen career path. Don't reinvent the wheel if you don't have to. Listen to them. They can help you.

Passion is a word we hear a lot. What's your passion? What makes you want to jump out of bed early on a Monday morning and attack the day? What makes you lose track of time but still leaves you energized at the end of a long day?

It's critically important that you be honest with yourself as you identify your true passion. Is it music? Is it art? Is it managing projects? Is it making money? Is it travel? Take a Career Assessment Test, review the results, and you should have a really good beginning point as you seek that dream job. And remember … if you love what you do, success, fulfillment and the appropriate amount of abundance will find its way to you. It's true. Always has been, always will be. Trust me.

Finally, avoid undue peer pressure. Your friends love you but they don't <u>always</u> know what's best for you. Listen to them but trust your own instincts and the guidance of mentors. Ultimately, it's you who has to be happy doing what you do.

How to Evaluate Your Results

Let's talk about evaluating your results from a Career Assessment Test.

So, what did you discover from your Career Assessment Recommendation? Did you learn something about yourself you never knew before? Or did you confirm what you already knew? Either way, you just completed a critically important step in identifying, pursuing and landing that dream job.

Now that you've completed an assessment and have some recommendations, it's time to take a <u>realistic</u> look at your professional options as we begin to narrow the focus on your career of choice.

It's very important that you think in terms of a <u>career</u>, not an industry. An industry is simply a backdrop, it's not what you'll actually be <u>doing</u> day-to-day. For instance, if your chosen career is in sales or in research, remember there are career opportunities in sales or research in virtually <u>everything</u> from architecture to zoology – A to Z! That's why we need to focus on what you want to <u>do</u> vs. the broader backdrop of an industry.

Study your Career Assessment Recommendations. Really think about them – especially if you discovered something unexpected. Discuss the results with your mentor or mentors. Get their feedback. Envision yourself in a career you may never have considered prior to taking the Assessment. Feel the excitement and the possibilities for growth, success and fulfillment.

CLAMPS

The process of identifying a job and a company that best suits your passions and desires can often feel overwhelming … but it doesn't need to. All you need to do is put the "CLAMPS" on and you'll quickly find aligning your dream career and your dream company actually becomes quite methodical.

What do I mean by CLAMPS? Well, CLAMPS is an acronym for Challenge, Lifestyle, Advancement, Money, Prestige and Stability.

Let's take a closer look …

Challenge … is the learning, support and training provided by a company. You're going to want this if you desire to grow within the organization.

Lifestyle is, quite simply, the number of hours you'll be expected to work each week, as well as what hours you'll be working – 9-to-5, early shift, late shift, things like that. Your hours have a direct impact on your lifestyle so you need to take this into consideration.

Advancement is how quickly you can realistically expect to earn promotions and take on new challenges; essentially, how soon you can begin moving up the ladder.

Money … do I need to explain that? Probably so. Keep in mind, if money is most important to you, you may not be enhancing your profession because you're chasing the financial reward vs. growing as a professional and making a meaningful contribution. Money is, obviously, very important but, ultimately, your love of your job is what will drive your success.

It's generally better to make less and be happy, than make more and regret your career choice or company choice.

"P" stands for prestige of your desired position, company and industry. Figure out how important this is to you but be aware prestige is purely an ego matter and based more on emotion than benefit. You can prosper and grow within any organization, no matter how obscure it might be.

And finally, Stability. How stable is the organization and the industry? Is the company growing? Is it financially stable? Is it in a growth industry that will continue to provide opportunities for advancement? These are important questions.

We recommend you sit down with pad and pen and do what we call "rank and rate". Be honest with yourself. Which of these six considerations are most important to you? Which ones are non-negotiable in your mind? Once you've done this, rank them in order of importance and pretty soon you'll have identified how a particular profession and company aligns with your desires.

Find a Mentor!

Next, start enlisting the help of others. Who in your circle of contacts can help you learn more about your career or choice and the opportunities in that career? Pull out a pad and pen, or fire up the laptop or PC and list them. Be sure to include their contact info … email address, phone numbers, that kind of thing.

Next, identify people who are already doing what you desire to do. Reach out to them, meet with them -- ideally, in person – and ask them for advice. Generally speaking, people who love what they do are very eager to share details of their career with others.

And if you can't think of anyone in your immediate circle of contacts who's actually doing what you want to do, talk to them anyway and ask them if <u>they</u> know of anyone in their circle of contacts. Then ask them to make an introduction on your behalf. One of the keys of success is to always ask. You want to live the old adage, "Ask and you will receive."

In real estate, experts always talk about "location, location, location". And in the landscape of career-building, it's all about "networking, networking, networking". You've already identified a mentor, or maybe more than one mentor. Now, it's time to identify a mentor specifically working in your chosen career. But be sure to find someone who's respected among peers and who's knowledgeable. This is the type of person who can give you the greatest insight and guidance and you journey towards that dream job.

Clean Up your Online Profile

Now it's time to make sure you're presenting yourself positively and professionally – especially on social networking websites.

Recent studies show that most of people already have a profile on at least one social networking site – Facebook, LinkedIn, Twitter, or any of the others. And did you know that 51% of these people fully expect employers or potential employers to check out their profile. It's true!

If you don't already understand this, now is the time to accept that your page or your profile absolutely paints a picture of you. The great Mark Twain once said "A person never gets a second chance to make a first impression." Hmmmm …

So make sure your first impression is appealing. Your profile on a social networking site is often your only chance to make a positive, first impression. Don't blow it!

Go online and review each one of your social networking site profiles. View them from the perspective of an employer or prospective employer. Take out any unprofessional or inappropriate images, comments, graphics, music, videos, whatever. You don't necessarily have to come across as a "goody-two-shoes" – I mean, we all have friends and we all like to have a good time – but be sure the balance of information available about you on your chosen social networking sites tells the real story of who you are, where your outside interests lie, where you've traveled, what you've accomplished, things like that. Things that will enhance your career prospects as you seek your dream job.

Next, reconsider your online circle of friends. You may have a soft spot for the good-hearted slacker who can't seem to keep a job or dress neatly but an employer or prospective employer may not like the fact that you hang with someone like this. Also, your friend might have inappropriate pics with you tagged. If true, either temporarily delete your friends or place your settings on a more confidential basis.

Is this fair? Probably not. Is it reality? You betcha!

So, reevaluate your online circle of friends and make sure the apparent company you keep reflects positively on you. Be honest and ask yourself "What does my online profile really say about me?"

OK, if you want an edge with your competition, it's time to clean it up!

Are Your Ready For The Second Commandment

So, let's take a quick look back as we prepare to move ahead to Commandment 2 in the process of finding you your dream job in your chosen career. In Commandment 1:

- You took a Career Assessment Test and identified some career choices
- You understand CLAMPS and which ones are important to you and which ones are nonnegotiable.
- You identified all-important internal and external contacts that you can lean on as you pursue your dream job in your career of choice.
- You've identified at least one respected and knowledgeable professional mentor already doing the type of job you desire.
- And you've tidied up all your social networking sites to make sure you're making a positive, <u>professional</u> first impression.

Wow … you've come a long way in just a short period of time! I think we're ready to move on to Commandment 2.

Congratulations!

COMMANDMENT TWO

Thou Shalt Craft The Tools Needed To Search

"Be strong and take heart, all you who hope in the Lord."
Psalm 31:24

What Is a Resume? Do I Really Need One?

Let's talk resume.

I know, I know … you're probably asking yourself *"Do I really need a resume'?"* Well, let me put it to you this way. A resume' alone will never land you a job. However … you will never find your dream job in your career of choice <u>without</u> a resume'. So let's get going' …

As you begin the process of creating your resume', you must understand that the true <u>purpose</u> of a resume' is, first and foremost, to generate interviews. It's not simply an opportunity to tell a story about you.

Next – and this may seem unbelievable but it's true – the average resume' gets about five seconds of consideration from a screener. Your resume' is going to make you or break you in just about the same amount of time it takes to say, "Hello, my name is …" Crazy but true. So this is serious stuff here.

Think about your resume' as a selling or marketing tool – and your skills and experience are the product being sold. In reviewing your resume', an employer wants to quickly determine one thing, do you meet the specifications of the job that's open? That's it. Nothing more.

Your resume' must be easy to read and appealing to the eye. Nobody wants to read a jumbled, rambling, overly text-heavy document so use ample white space and be succinct in your wording.

Additionally, your resume' should carry keywords that match the desired attributes and qualifications listed in the job description to capture the attention and interest of the person screening or reviewing resumes'. You should consider having a resume for each career field. For example, Human Resources, Marketing, etc. Your keywords, work history, etc. should then reflect the wording and your experience in the specific field.

Next -- and you've probably heard it your entire life -- <u>Always tell the truth. Period.</u> Trust me, it pays off in the end! Don't include any false information because it will be uncovered and you'll regret it later. Tell the truth.

So, before we move on, understand that a resume' is a bit of a paradox. It's critically important yet it's only a small part of finding a dream job. It's kinda like your car key. It's not the most important component of your car but, without it, you'll get nowhere.

Different Types of Resumes

OK, you've accepted the harsh reality that a resume' is important so the next question is: What kind of resume' is best for me? Well, let's take a closer look ...

There are several types of resumes. Most popular are ...
- Chronological, which lists your work history, by date
- Functional, which groups your background by skill, activities or accomplishments
- Curriculum Vitae, which is used to highlight extensive academic and professional credentials, and is used mostly often by educators and scientists

The Chronological resume' is generally the most popular format for job-seekers and employers because it's easiest to follow and understand.

So, identify which resume' will best showcase your skills and accomplishments and let's start filling in the blanks.

Summary Objective

You've decided on a resume' style so what's the next step? Well, it's determining whether or not you need an objective at the head of your resume' or a summary. So, what's the difference?

Well, an "objective" tells the resume' reviewer what <u>type</u> of position or career you desire and what <u>skills</u> you have to support this goal or direction. And a "summary" is just that – a "summarized" sales pitch of your area of interest, based on your work experience, background, skills, and education.

They're similar yet distinct in a very subtle way. And it's up to you to decide which approach will best support your desire to land that dream job. Whichever direction you choose, understand that your "objective" or "summary" must be clear, direct, eye-catching, intriguing and written in a brief paragraph format. This is a case of "less is more". Keep it brief, concise and clear so you set the stage for a review of your skills and accomplishments.

Accomplishments

Let's talk about accomplishments, <u>your</u> accomplishments. Today is the perfect day for you to sit quietly with a pad and pen and list those areas and times of your life where and when you've made a mark … in school, in a previous job, with volunteer groups, in community activities, within other organizations, and so forth. What are some of the things you're <u>most</u> proud of?

Now, let's develop bullet points that highlight these achievements and accomplishments in a clear and concise manner. Wherever possible, quantify the accomplishments by incorporating dollar amounts, percentages, numbers and results. This gives substance and credence to what you did well. Facts Sell! So, rather than say, "I increased sales and was a leader in the company" it is better to say, "I increased sales by 19% and as a results was among the top 5% out of 300 in the company."

As for tone, hey, this is <u>your</u> time to shine -- your moment onstage -- and it may just be the one shot you have to move to the next level of consideration as you pursue your dream job. And it's OK to brag a little. After all, it's <u>your</u> accomplishment. <u>You</u> own it. Just don't go overboard and declare yourself the greatest thing since sliced bread (or the iPod, for that matter).

Be sure to tell your story with impact and be sure to select accomplishments from the list you jotted down that an employer or prospective employer can most easily translate into a benefit for <u>their</u> company. After all – and this is very important and sometimes a little tough to swallow – but, right now, it's all about the employer, <u>not</u> you. It's all about what <u>you</u> can do for <u>them</u>. <u>Your</u> time will come a little later.

<u>Employment History</u>

Now it's time to build the Employment History section.

Go in reverse chronological order – that is, work backward from today --- and begin with your current or most recent place of employment. Include your job title, a brief job description that identifies your roles and responsibilities, and use an bullet point format for clarity.

Be sure to list internships and any volunteer work you've done (a lot of employers or prospective employers truly value volunteer work and "giving back"). And if there were time gaps in your employment history, find a way to explain those gaps in a positive manner. For instance, you might say "in between my time with Acme Corporation and Jones Construction, I spent three months tutoring elementary school students in reading and math". This helps shift the attention from a period of unemployment and presents it as a period of personal growth and achievement.

Finally, be sure to include 2-3 of your meaningful accomplishments in each specific position.

So grab that pen and paper, sit down and start looking back at all the great things you've <u>already</u> accomplished in the jobs you've had. Then build 'em into that resume' of yours that's looking stronger and stronger all the time. You're on your way!

<u>Education</u>

Now it's time to make all those late nights cramming for exams or writing term papers go to work for you on your resume'.

Your education … you earned it so let's highlight it.

When it comes to educational background, what is an employer or prospective employer <u>really</u> looking for? Well, it is four things: the type of degree you earned (or are about to earn), your major field of study, your minor or minors, and your GPA. Here's an example of how you might list your educational background …

- *West Virginia State University   May 2009*
- *Bachelor of Science*
- *Major: Business Administration – Human Resource Management*
- *Minor: Speech Communications*
- *GPA: 3.9 (on 4.0 scale)*

But employers and prospective employers are also looking for any additional courses, training, honors or certifications in your background that further enhance your credentials for employment.

In most cases, the more well-rounded you are, the more appealing you are as a candidate for that dream job. So, again, this is no time to be overly modest. Tell them about your awards or outside training or certifications. Tell them how you went on a mission trip to Central America. Tell them how you're Red Cross-certified to teach CPR. Tell them how you took a computer skills training seminar while on summer break before your senior year. These are important pieces of the puzzle. You worked at these and they definitely contribute to the wonderful package of skills and experience you're offering.

Activities and Groups

It's said that education takes place <u>outside</u> the confines of a classroom as much as <u>within</u> the four walls of a classroom. How true is that!

As an employer or prospective employer reviews your resume', he or she is, of course, interested in the details of your formal education. But perhaps just as importantly, they want to know what else you have done outside of your education and employment. In many cases, this reveals more about you as a person – and as an employment candidate – than anything else.

It paints a more complete picture of who you are, where your interests lie, and how deeply committed you are to causes, activities and your chosen career. Your membership in organizations may give you an edge over candidates you're competing with. For instance, a role as an on-campus, student advocate for Habitat for Humanity may differentiate you from others in a very positive way.

An elected or officer position in groups or organizations such as a fraternity or sorority demonstrates leadership abilities. And leadership is certainly a skill that's transferable to any employer or prospective employer.

Be sure to list all activities supportive of your desired field. Let me give you an example: If you were a Journalism major with an emphasis in Media Relations, be sure to list that you were <u>also</u> a member of the Public Relations Student Society of America for three years. This shows that you've already taken steps towards honing your craft outside the classroom and demonstrates a commitment to your chosen career field.

You can also draw from academic groups, professional associations, sports activities, community outreach programs, church-based activities, and so on.

Your participation in activities or groups shows focus, involvement and that you have the ability to make a difference. Good for you! Now, use those activities and associations as a way to gain the inside track in the race for your ultimate quest.

Cover Letters

Now that your formal resume' is complete, there are a couple more elements to the resume' package that you will need. The first is a cover letter.

You may be asking if a cover letter is necessary when submitting your resume online or by "snail mail". Yes and yes! This is your opportunity for a pre-emptive strike, your chance to state right up-front "what makes you right for the job".

Your cover letter must do four things. It must: spark the interest of the reviewer, get them to look (or look more closely) at your resume, briefly identify your interests, and succinctly summarize your qualifications for the job you desire. That's a lot. And that's why the cover letter is so critically important.

In terms of format, err to the side of formality when it comes to salutations and closings. You may know that Mary Jones is the hiring manager but she's Ms. Jones to you until you've been given permission to be less formal. Your signoff should be equally professional.

How long should a cover letter be? Not long, but not too short, either. In 3-4 succinct paragraphs, you must identify the position you are applying for and state your sincere interest ... state what makes you the right candidate for the job ... express your gratitude for being considered ... and provide your contact information and planned follow-up step (such as, I will follow-up with a phone call by such-and-such date).

One final note ...

In today's tech-reliant times when resume's are zapped around the world via the internet, the good ol' fashioned cover letter is still necessary. No matter how you deliver your resume' – online or via "snail mail" – craft a cover letter.

Professional References

Alright, you've completed your resume', you've written the greatest cover letter known to man, and now you need to be ready to provide an employer or prospective employer a list of Professional References. But who are these "professional references"?

In short, they're people willing to go to bat for you, and who have the ability to add some topspin and pizzazz to your chances of landing that dream job ... you know, the one you're moving closer and closer to with each step.

Your professional references should be able to attest to your skills, your abilities, and your accomplishments. These include people you've worked for – or worked <u>with</u> – in the past. These are people who've seen you in action and can sing your praises.

But, be careful. When jotting down potential professional references, you must be 100% sure the information and perspective they share will be favorable to you. If there's even a shred of doubt, strike them from your list!

Once you're comfortable with your list, be courteous and let each person know that you would like to get their permission to use them as a reference. You might even ask them if they'd be willing to provide you a reference in writing. If this is a previous or current employer, ask that the letter of reference be printed on company letterhead.

As each person agrees to be your professional reference, ask them to notify you if they are called by the company you desire to work for – and thank them afterward! This is very important.

Your formalized list of professional references should include each person's name, company, address, contact number, email address and position or title.

Finally, be prepared to present your professional references (in hard copy form or as a file attachment to an email) immediately upon request by your employer or prospective employer.

Are You Ready For The Third Commandment?

You're rockin' and rollin' now! You've taken a Career Assessment Test, identified a career, built your network and, by completing Commandment 2:

- You understand the purpose of a resume' is to generate interviews
- You've created a great chronological resume' that highlights your skills and accomplishments in the context of your employer or prospective employer's current needs
- You've written a brilliant cover letter that comes alive!
- And you've formalized a list of professional references that have given you permission to use their names and contact info.

Career choice, check!

Resume', check!

Cover letter, check!

Professional references, check!

Do you realize how much ground you've covered already? Good for you!

But there's still more work to be done so let's move on to The Third Commandment.

COMMANDMENT THREE

Thou Shalt Walk Softly Among The Advertised Openings

"There is surely a future hope for you, and your
hope will not be cut off."
Prov. 23:18

A x E x E = R

Let's talk about a secret formula.

A x E x E = R … are we channeling our inner Albert Einstein here? Not really. This is just a simple equation that may well turn out to be *your* secret formula for success as you pursue that dream job.

A x E x E = R stands for … Attitude x Exposure x Efficiency= Results

Let's break it down …

Your attitude … a wise man once said "Whether you think you can … or you can't, you're right!" As anyone who has ever "made it" will tell you, the glass simply *can't* be half-empty. It *has* to be full and you *have* to believe it will *soon* be overflowing! Attitude is everything so choose a positive one.

Exposure … job-shopping is a numbers game. You've got to get out there, get out there, get out there. Interview, interview, interview. Network, network, network. You simply can't expect to hit 50 homeruns if you only go to bat five times so exposure is critical. You have to give yourself many opportunities to succeed in your quest. And remember … the only time you truly fail is the last time you tried!

Efficiency ... comes from exposure and learning. Repetition makes you better in virtually everything you do in life, including job-seeking. You should <u>also</u> ask the pros what you can do better so that your efforts are constantly advancing and your skills are enhanced because, if you're not better today than you were yesterday, your learning has stopped and you'll quickly become stagnant.

And results ... no explaining needed.

<u>Advertised Openings</u>

It's time to take a look at some of the sources for job leads you'll likely be using. There are essentially five sources for job postings – job boards, traditional newspapers, online newspapers, third-party recruiters, and company websites.

With job boards, it's important for you to set up search agents that lead to daily or weekly updates. Though not the best way to source job leads, traditional newspapers are still loaded with "help wanted" entries on a daily basis. If you read newspapers online, be sure to identify which day of the week new ads are typically placed and get there first!

If you're dealing with third-party recruiters, limit your options to recruiters who specialize in your area of interest or you may find yourself simply spinning your wheels. Once you do locate a recruiter in your field send them a resume' and call them directly and ask for an interview, their advice and who else they know that you can contact. It is all about being **PROACTIVE**!

More and more, company websites are adding job openings, usually under the "careers" tab or via a link to another website.

Searching for job leads must be a disciplined pursuit so it's important that you schedule time to apply for advertised openings each week. However, do not let it consume an inordinate amount of your job-search time. You should spend no more than a few hours each week checking these resources.

Lastly, hang in there when you're dealing with these resources. It's a numbers game and it can be a long one. Studies show it could take as many as 1,500 resumes' distributed before you even get an offer. That's a lot of effort but this book will show you a better way!

Job Boards

Let's talk a little more about job boards. If this is a job-search approach you choose to utilize, understand that the process may be relatively easy but the approach is largely ineffective. Studies reveal that only a small percentage of all jobs are filled through postings on job boards. Essentially, this is a **reactive approach vs. a pro-active approach**. I am not saying don't use job boards, just that it is important to know the facts. Taking a reactive approach makes you "one of many" vs. being a member of "the chosen few". Bottom line: it's rare that anyone ever finds their dream job on a job board.

However, if you choose to go this route, the first thing you must do is establish your own, personal job seeker account. In your account, you'll set up job search agents. You'll likely need to develop several job search agents to maximize your chances of making a connection with a job opening that suits your desired career opportunity.

Next, you'll need to post a resume and cover letter – yes, a cover letter is necessary. Be sure to attach different resume's for different career fields. Also, your resumes will need to be "search friendly"; that is, it should reflect your area of interest. Use keywords that correlate to the type of job description that appeals to you. To identify these keywords, review a number of job postings and pick and choose those words that are appropriate for your resume.

Finally, stay current! Update or edit your resume' on a weekly basis to ensure it gets searched and discovered more frequently. The more you update it, the more likely it is your resume' will be among the first to be searched. Updating may be as simple as changing 2-3 words, using synonyms which allow you to change the wording but not the thought.

Targeting a Bulls-Eye Employer List

It's time to prepare for your journey into cyberspace to find the job you desire. There are definitely some steps that must be taken before you enter the vastness of the internet.

First, you must develop a "Targeted Employer List". This shifts the way you go about your search because you're now in the mode of <u>making</u> something happen vs. <u>waiting</u> for something to happen (like with job boards). Be sure to include all companies of interest to you.

Next, you need to research these companies thoroughly by reading online news items about the company, visiting the company website, speaking to people who work – or have worked – at companies you're targeting.

Your list of what we call "bull's-eye employers" should include at least 20 companies to in order to increase your chances of finding that dream job. As you research various employers, utilize Moody's Industrial Manual, Hoovers, Google, local chambers of commerce, etc. Seek ways to learn more about each employer so when you do get that call for an interview, you're prepared. Use some type of system to keep track of your employer list.

Another great way to conduct research is to attend networking events as well as utilizing social networking sites. These sites can help you identify key people within a targeted organization, how to reach them and perhaps provide some informational tidbits about that person that can be used to your benefit when you do connect with them.

Company Websites

Let's talk for a moment about company websites and how best to use them to uncover job opportunities. Most employers place advertised openings in the "Careers" section of their website <u>before</u> they place them on generic job boards so this is a search technique that often helps the early bird get the worm.

You should review your Targeted Bulls-eye Employer List and visit those companies' websites frequently since job openings pop up on a daily basis. Yesterday's listings may be totally different than today's but you won't know if you don't go.

Create an advantage over your competition by using www.Watchthatpage.com. This website automatically sends you emails, alerting you to changes on website pages. Go to the company's career section of their website. Narrow your search to your specific field. Then simply copy the URL of the page into your Watch That Page account. As soon as there is a change on that website page, Watch That Page notifies you. This can be very helpful and give you the inside track once a new opportunity is posted.

However, if there <u>are</u> no openings posted that appeal to you, or in the absence of a previous introduction, do <u>not</u> send out resumes blindly. It's a waste of time – yours and theirs. You need to wait on an actual posting then identify who within the organization is accepting resume's for that particular position. It's very, very important that you manage <u>who</u> gets your resume and <u>how</u> it is distributed.

Resume Metrics & Tracking

"It's very, very important that you manage who gets your resume and how it is distributed." Why? Well, let's take a closer look …

The greater the number of resumes' distributed directly to targeted contacts, the greater the chances are you will actually get an interview. This is really a no-brainer. Simply put, if you want to fish, you have to go where the fish are.

You should also send a minimum of 25 resumes per week to targeted contacts. That may sound like a lot – and it is – but it will also help you find that dream job sooner so it's worth the effort.

Another important tool to use is some type of tracking device. It can be as simple as a pad of paper or an excel sheet. But you will need a tracking system which allows you to track positions for which you've already applied, key contact persons, companies you've submitted resumes' to, and when you applied for a particular position.

Are You Ready For Commandment 4

Alright, before you move on to Commandment 4, let's quickly review what you've learned in Commandment 3.

- You now understand the various sources for advertised openings
- You realize that, while easy to use, job boards are not the most efficient way to find your dream job. But if you choose to use job boards, use them properly.
- You've created a Targeted Bulls-eye Employer List of at least 20 companies
- You know how to research company websites for pre-job board openings
- You're targeting who gets your resume and how it is distributed
- You're going to distribute a minimum of 25 resumes per week
- And you're using a Tracking System to organize and manage names, companies, contact info, etc.

This is really moving along. I'm proud of you! Now, let's proceed to Commandment 4.

COMMANDMENT

FOUR

Thou Shalt Be Proactive Versus Reactive

"Be diligent in these matters; give yourself wholly to them, so that everyone may see your progress."

I Timothy 4:15

Inbound vs. Outbound Calls

Lets address phone etiquette, voicemails and live interaction at Job Fairs; those points of … "contact" … you will certainly have as you move closer and closer to landing that dream job. Let's begin …

First of all, let me share a very important statistic with you. There are different ways you can conduct your job search but it's important that you understand, when you apply for a job and sit back and wait for the next step, over 80% of the job opportunities will pass you by. In essence, you might have a shot at one of every five openings. Those aren't good odds.

That's why it's so critical that you <u>make</u> it happen versus <u>let</u> it happen. How do you do this? Well, there are three ways … you can apply and follow-up with a call … you can call then follow up with an application … or you can make a call and choose <u>not</u> to apply if you discover the opportunity just isn't the right fit for you and what you're seeking. And that's OK.

In any event, you <u>must</u> be pro-active and <u>drive</u> the process vs. letting the process drive <u>you</u>.

Your Telephone Voice

Let's talk about phone calls. Incoming calls, in particular, because, at some point in your search for a job, you're going to receive a phone call or numerous phone calls from a prospective employer or hiring manager.

Rule No. 1 -- always be ready for the call! What does this mean? Well, be sure you take the call in a quiet environment so you can pay close attention to what's being said and so the caller doesn't feel distracted. If the call comes in and you need to step outside or into another room, do it.

Next, don't take the call until you've silenced all background music or televisions. In fact, turn the TV <u>off</u> so you're not visually distracted. And that yappy dog of yours? Uh-uh. They don't belong anywhere within earshot when you're discussing what just might be your biggest career break ever. Moms, Dads, and babysitters, this goes for crying babies, too. And finally, no running water or dishwasher in the background. Turn 'em off before you take the call.

All of these things can be annoying and distracting and could drop you right out of the running for that dream job.

Inbound Calls from Potential Employers

Now, let's talk more specifically about incoming calls.

First of all, be sure your voicemail message sounds professional, friendly and articulate. If you need to, script out a greeting and read from this script as you record your voicemail greeting. Remember, it may not be a live point-of-contact but it's a point-of-contact nonetheless. Make sure it sounds positive!

Secondly, always be <u>ready</u> for "The Call". When you're looking for a job, you've got to anticipate that call coming in at any time of day, any day of the week. You never know when it will take place.

Before blindly answering your phone, check you're Caller ID so you can move to a quieter environment, silence distracting background noises, and take a deep breath to prepare yourself. If you don't recognize the number, assume it's a hiring manager or prospective employer and answer professionally.

Finally, track your calls. Use a tracking system, which can be as simple as a pad of paper or an excel sheet to readily identify the caller, callers company and what time, what date and what was discussed – especially any follow-up steps.

Outbound Calls to Employers – Applying For a Job Posting

Many times <u>you</u> will be the one initiating a phone call to discuss a specific job opening. So how should you prepare?

First, be sure to review any company research you've gathered so the information is top-of-mind for you. Secondly, thoroughly reread the job posting and understand the details of it. Next, follow your greeting and introduction script so you don't stumble or stammer when you're just getting started.

Your greeting and introduction script should include: who you are, why you are calling and what you want.

So for example: Hi Mr. Employer. My name is Dave, The reason for my call is I am would like to apply for the job posting for a (whatever). I have done (link your skills to the skills specified in the job posting).

And before you conclude your phone call, you must ask two very important questions …

"What are the next steps?", and …

"What can I do to maximize my chances to make it to the next level of consideration?"

Outbound Calls to Employer – How to Follow-Up After You Submit An Application

OK, you've submitted an application for a posted job and now it's time to follow-up with a phone call. M<u>aking</u> it happen vs. <u>letting</u> it happen? That's what we're doing here.)

First and quite obviously, locate the proper number to call. When the person on the other end answers, politely and professionally ask to be transferred to the Human Resources Department. Once the call has been transferred to HR, ask the person who answers for the name of the HR recruiter or hiring manager responsible for filling the position <u>you're</u> interested in.

If, by chance, they won't divulge this information, refer to Commandment 6 – Social Networking – to assist you in finding alternative ways to identify specific hiring managers.

And perhaps most importantly, speak with an energy and passion when you've got someone on the phone. People naturally gravitate to others who sound positive and friendly so be sure <u>you</u> do!

Talking to a Live HR Person

Alright, <u>bingo</u>! You've managed to be connected to the HR recruiter or hiring manager who's handling the job <u>you</u> desire. Now what?

First, begin by introducing yourself by name and state the exact title of the position you desire. Politely ask for the status of the application.

Also be sure to ask the person, "If you were me, what would <u>you</u> do to get an interview?" And if you don't feel you've gotten a helpful answer, take a second shot at it. Remember, like we said at the beginning of Step 4 – this is a contact sport! Ask them, "What <u>else</u> can I do to maximize my chances of making it to the next round of consideration?"

You'll probably get something helpful when you do this.

Voice Mail To Human Resources

If you strike out and don't get a <u>live</u> voice on the other end of the phone and you're directed into voicemail, be sure to leave a concise, professional and friendly message.

Begin by saying your name and then spelling it – and spell it slowly enough so the person has time to jot it down when they pick up the message. Next, state your phone number and repeat <u>it</u> slowly enough so, <u>again</u>, they can easily jot down the number. The last thing you want is to be dropped from consideration because they couldn't understand your phone number when you spoke too fast or not clearly enough. This may seem obvious but its <u>incredible</u> how many people make this mistake.

Next, state <u>why</u> you're calling and <u>when</u> you submitted your application for the posted opening. Reference the opening by using the <u>exact</u> title taken from the job posting.

Briefly and enthusiastically express your interest in the position and, as you wrap up, restate your name and phone number and close in a friendly fashion with something like "I look forward to chatting with you" or "I look forward to your return call."

Making Job Fairs Work 4U

Alright, you've heard about a Job Fair going on in your area and you want to attend. So how should you prepare since this is a great opportunity for a face-to-face point-of-contact. There are things that you should do and there are definitely things you should not do if you want to make a Job Fair work for you.

Let's take a look at what you should do first …

Begin by sitting down and writing your 30-second "elevator pitch". If you're not familiar with this term, basically, it's being able to effectively deliver your own personal "sales pitch" in the 30 seconds you might share with another person on an elevator who's interested in you and what you're seeking. Write it, time it, and rehearse it. And after you're done rehearsing it, rehearse it a few more times! This is your chance to shine during a quick point-of-contact.

Next, be sure to bring an ample supply of your business cards with you to the Job Fair. The last thing you want to do is run out then have someone ask you for a card. This would be a missed opportunity to make a positive impression.

Speaking of business cards, be sure to include your name, address, email address, and phone number. And here is another advantage tip. You can use the back of the business card to advertise yourself. You should include accomplishments or achievements that you are proud of from your resume.

Along with your fully rehearsed "elevator pitch" and your business cards, be sure to bring a number of updated, clean copies of your resume'.

In terms of appropriate attire, think of the Job Fair as a job interview – **because it is**. You should wear a conservative suit – preferably dark in color during the Fall and Winter months and lighter colors in Spring and Summer months. Your shoes should be clean and polished ... and no from sandals or flip-flops.

Once you arrive at the Job Fair, be sure to take job posting flyers off each table you visit. On your interview, be sure to use some of the information on the flyers such as the company motto, mission statement or what the company stands for. Make sure to align their beliefs with yours.

Here is a tip. Instead of just getting in line go to the side of the booth and quietly pick up some information on the table. While there, take a few steps back and listen to some of the questions the employer is asking in the interview in front of you. Then you can be prepared to answer the same questions yourself. The more you do this, the more you will have a competitive advantage.

Next, be sure to get business cards from everyone you speak to.

And after the Job Fair, you must follow-up within 24 hours with a handwritten thank-you note – which is considered the most personal approach – or with a phone call or email to the people you spoke with. Following up in a timely fashion is yet another opportunity for you to demonstrate your professionalism and make a positive impression.

Now, let's take a look at what you should not do when attending a Job Fair …

In terms of attire, no casual outfits – never! You don't want to look as if you just decided to "pop in" on your way home. This will backfire on you, trust me.

Next, don't show up with soiled, wrinkled or crumpled copies of your resume'.

And even if you feel like you've made an immediate, friendly connection with a person at the Job Fair, avoid coming across as overly relaxed or having an attitude that's too casual. Also avoid conversation involving personal matters or any non-job-related topics. They call it a Job Fair and not a cocktail party for a reason!

As we said earlier, treat a Job Fair like a job interview – because it is!

Are You Ready For Commandment 5?

Well, we're almost ready to move on to Commandment 5 which deals with Traditional Networking but, before we do, let's quickly summarize what we've covered in Commandment 4.

You now know how to prepare for inbound and outbound phone calls and the importance of using a professional voice. We covered inbound calls from potential employers as well as the importance of and how to initiate calls to employers.

You also know the appropriate way to make a follow-up phone call to a potential employer after an application has been submitted and how to interact once you have a live person on the other end of the phone.

And, of course, these days it's all-too-common that your call kicks into voicemail so we covered the proper way to leave a succinct, professional and friendly voicemail message.

Finally, we reviewed what you should do and should not do when preparing for and participating in a Job Fair. And, make sure you have a great 30-second "elevator pitch".

Wow, we covered a lot of ground. I believe you're ready to move to Commandment 5.

Good luck!

COMMANDMENT

FIVE

Thou Shalt Covet Your Neighbors Connections

"Cast your bread upon the waters, for after many
days you will find it again."
Eccl. 11:1

What Is Networking and Why Is It Important to Finding a Job?

You know that networking is really important when it comes to being able to find a job and help you in your job search process.

Here's a statistic for you: Did you know that 80% of all new jobs are found through networking? And if that wasn't bad enough, did you know that out of all the jobs that are out there, 50% of them are actually unadvertised. Meaning they weren't on a website, they weren't on a career board and you weren't able to find them at a job fair.

You see the key with finding a job with some of these unadvertised positions is being able to network and engage with the hiring managers or key level executives.

Think of it this way... a lot of times when you're working on a company, you'll talk with the HR person. And the HR person might say to you, "we've got your application but unfortunately we don't have a job for you". Or, they might tell you, "we've got your application and we have a job, but you're number 129 on that list".

Yet, when you're talking to a hiring level manager, what that person is able to do is say, "we've got your application and we're going to be able to find a job that's going to be a fit for you as it relates to your specific skills and expertise that you bring to the table". They can literally create a position for you.

You know, a great quote that I heard one time was, "Never take no from someone who doesn't have the authority to tell you yes". And that is so important when it comes to networking.

Now remember, when you're networking...its going to go exponentially. Meaning, as you get a chance to know more people in the community, your reputation is going to get out there and that's going to make the job search a whole lot easier.

Networking Groups

Now what we're going to talk about are the top three networking groups that you really do need to be a part of. We're going to do it in a countdown fashion.

So, number three is going to be service clubs. Now if you're not familiar with a service club, it's real easy. We're talking about places like the Kiwanis club, the rotary club. These are organizations that meet on a weekly basis, usually for lunch…sometimes for breakfast. And they are very civic-oriented.

Now what you are going to get from these groups is usually a little older crowd. You might find some people who are retirees or are already working or doing other things in the community. But the reason I like this so much is because individuals in service clubs, by definition, are service oriented. This means that they will be more willing to help you network and find organizations that can help you find a job.

Number two is going to be alumni associations. Now, when it comes to alumni associations, there are really only three things that you need to remember. It's all about relationships, follow-up, and passing out and gathering as many business card as you can.

Now, lets back up to why we like alumni associations… They obviously have a bond with you. They went to the school with you, you've graduated from that same school and now you have an opening to talk to people who are already working and they can help you network into those same organizations.

And number one is trade associations. Now you may not be familiar with a trade organization. That's real easy. You have an accounting association, you have a marketing association, you have an engineering association. Every functioning group that you're a part of has a national association that is associated with it. What you need to do is be able to go on to Google and type in "national association of..." and now what you'll be able to do is find a group that meets in your local area.

How To Stand Out From The Crowd

We're going to talk a little bit about creating a visible identity. A visible identity is really important when it comes to networking and being able to stand out from the crowd in meeting other people.

Now, if you haven't heard that term before, it is really easy. A visible identity simply asks, how can you differentiate yourself in the mind of one person from the other five people that they've already met. You see, this is something that's going to be really important when you're interviewing. It will be important when you have your resumes, and obviously it will be important when you're out networking.

Now let me set the stage for you here a little bit. You're at an alumni event and you're out meeting people. What you want to do is demonstrate that you are actually out there trying to help them. When you go to these events, people are all "gimme gimme gimme" and we don't want to come across like that. So what you have to do is ask the right questions while you're out there networking.

One of them is you want to be able to ask people "where else do you normally network?"

Ok, great question to be able to move the process forward. They'll tell you a little bit about themselves and it's a great way to do things.

Second question, you might ask what they do. They might ask a little about what you do. I like to ask "What do you like best about what you do?" Then from there ask them question number three. Ask them "how did they get started in that direction".

You put these questions together and you will absolutely be able to stand out from the crowd and be able to show that you care.

Now, I'll even give you a little bonus question… "If you were me, who are three people that you think I should meet". That is a great way to get you moving to do what it is that you need to do.

How To Explain What Your Do In A Unique Way

A little bit about a unique selling proposition and how that can help you stand out from the crowd. If you've never heard of a unique selling proposition, it simply tells people what you do in a manner that makes them ask how you do it.

When you're out networking, a lot of times people are going to ask you "what do you do". And the answer is not "oh well I'm looking for a job in engineering" but rather "I'm looking to work for an organization that's dedicated towards producing exceptional quality work in the field of engineering". Now that might be a little lengthy but you get the idea.

The important thing is that you want to be able to have it where you take some of the benefits that you bring to the table and put that in a sentence or response so they are able to see you in a different light.

Now, let me give you another example. If you were looking for a marketing job, you wouldn't just say, "I'm trying to find a marketing job". You would say, "I'm looking to work with a forward thinking organization to help them effectively market and brand their company". You see how that gives you a little something to help you stand out from the crowd?

Mastering the Coffee Connection

This is really where the heavy lifting comes along in your networking because it is where you're able to turn a lot of these contacts that you get during networking events into bottom line results in your job search.

Now, naturally the question is, "what is a coffee connection"? It's real easy. It is simply a meeting at a place of your choice where you're able to have some coffee with that person that you just met at the networking event. You get a chance to learn a little more about what they do and they can find out a little bit about what you do in order to strengthen and develop the relationship.

So here's what you do while you're having a coffee connection. First off, you're going to a networking event and you want to create a visible identity with everyone you meet. And if you can, schedule some times and dates with people while you're there networking for that coffee connection. For everyone else, you're going to want to send out an email that invites them to your local coffee shop.

Now, what will that email say? It could say something along the lines of "Hi, my name is _____. We met at the alumni association a couple days ago and I was hoping we could get together for a quick cup of coffee to talk about your business and some of the things that I do. I'm pretty booked this week (your always booked this week) but I was hoping we could get together next week for coffee.

Alright now, from there you will find that about 40% of the people will respond to your email right there and voila! You'll be getting coffee with them. For the people that don't respond to your email, you'll want to pick up the phone and you're going to want to give them a call and say "Hey listen, we met at this event. I'd like to talk to you a little bit about your business and move forward from there".

Regardless of how you do it, here's the important thing to remember when you're networking ... you absolutely need to have some goals in mind when it comes to going to a networking event, when it comes to being able to have at least 2-3 coffee connections from that networking event so that you can move things forward.

Got Goals?

Now that we've put out all this great information as it relates to networking, let's spend a minute getting organized on exactly what your networking expectations should be throughout a normal week.

I'm going to suggest you attend at least one professional networking event per week. This could be a service club, alumni meeting, or even a trade association. We just need one event each week to get up and active within a networking community.

From there, I need you to create a visible identity with at least five people at the event. Now, that's not nearly as hard as it may sound because now you're armed with some questions on what you can ask while networking as well as an engaging unique.

Are You Ready For Commandment 6?

As we get ready to move to Commandment 6 which deals with Social Networking let's quickly capture what was covered in Commandment 5.

- Per week: Attend 1 professional networking event, create 5 visible identities at each event, 3 coffee connections.

- Nothing gets done while you're sitting in the house. The real heavy lifting comes from physically meeting new people.

- Know that many positions are created due to a match of a job seeker with a hiring authority who wasn't thinking of hiring initially

- "Never take a no from someone who cannot give you a yes."

- The key is to network with upper level executives.

- Ask everyone, "If you were me, who are three people do you think I should meet?"

- Joined networking associations and groups in your field.

- Do create a Visible Identity with everyone you meet.

- Do have a solid Unique Selling Proposition.

- Don't approach the networking process like an exercise in speed dating.

- And finally, do follow up with everyone you meet.

COMMANDMENT SIX

Honor But Use Social Networking Information To Your Advantage

"But those who hope in the Lord will renew their strength. They will soar on wings like eagles, they will run and not grow weary, they will walk and not be faint."

Isaiah 40:31

What is Social Networking?

Let's shift gears from traditional networking to the huge phenomenon known as <u>social</u> networking. The number of people connecting on LinkedIn, Facebook, Twitter and all the others is massive.

What was once just a trendy online activity is has become mainstream just as the internet has become mainstream over the past decade. Social networking is really huge … it's growing … and it's very likely here to stay so it's important that you use it in your efforts to land that dream job.

Like traditional networking, <u>social</u> networking depends on interactions between people through discussion and integration of words to build shared-meaning. The <u>biggest</u> difference is the fact that social networking relies on technology – that is, free, downloadable software programs and internet access.

There are five fundamental uses of social networking – communication between multiple parties, collaboration with others, posting multi-media files, sharing reviews and opinions for others to read, and entertainment.

So that's a quick snapshot of social networking in its simplest form. Now, let's take a closer look at how you can best put it to use in your job search.

Why Social Networking Is Important In Securing a Job?

Well, it makes your personal brand – that would be <u>you</u> – visible on the internet which is very, very important these days. And it's just as important for you to be honest and ask what your personal brand looks like online.

HR professionals are actively using social networking sites to search for and validate potential applicants. The HR types are out there looking, so why not be sure they find <u>you</u> and all that <u>you</u> have to offer with <u>your</u> skills and experience?

But the key is to be found easily. Specifically, you want your name and information about you to pop up on the very first page of an internet search because statistics show that resources appearing on the <u>first</u> page are the most likely to get scrutiny and attention from the person conducting the search. This is no time to be buried deep down on the search results.

Generally speaking, when it comes to getting in front of a hiring manager, personal introductions, networking and conversations are absolutely necessary because more than 80% of job placements come through networking – and these days, that includes social networking. And <u>that's</u> why it's so important.

It's all about getting interviews.

How to Use Social Networking to Secure Interviews

Your first step is to spend some time and thought and grow your network connections on LinkedIn®, Facebook®, Twitter® and others to get your personal brand out there. Who should you be friends with or have a connection with or be followed by?

Determine the organizations you want to work for and then find and link with connections from those companies, or with those who know people from those companies.

Secondly, use the search process and introduction tools on LinkedIn® to identify leaders of companies you've targeted.

Next, begin requesting and getting linked with those people.

You can also get people to follow you on Twitter®, so that your messages and ideas are being heard.

And on Facebook®, grow your list of friends to have access to decision-makers from companies where you might want to work.

So access your social networking sites <u>now</u> and start building that network of friends, connections and followers! Get Linked!

Nothing however beats direct physical contact. Once linked or introduced to a contact, let's try to call them directly. That's making it happen versus hoping it is going to occur.

Google the company and locate the phone number and then prepare to make your call.

When we reach them or leave a voice mail, thank them for linking with you and share with them some common interests that you obtained from their profile. Now is the time to use your 30-second elevator pitch again.

Finally … network, network, network. It's the name of the game and you should never stop growing your network and circle of influence. It's as important as flossing daily so do it!

Using Social Networking to Obtain Information That Can Be Used in an Interview

Let's take a look at how to use social networking sites to obtain information that can be helpful to you once you do land that interview at a targeted company.

First of all, be diligent and search for current and former employees of target companies to gain insight about the company and its future. When you do connect with those people, ask questions on Twitter®, Facebook®, LinkedIn® and the other sites to mine for information; that is, to get more details about the company, its management, annual goals and objectives, etc.

You can also use these sites to search for information like sales performance, P&L, or profit & loss statements, current issues, or any other important facts that <u>you</u> need to know to be best prepared for that first interview.

Finally, be sure to research the social networking profiles of HR or Hiring Managers to understand their management style, traits, personal interests and any information that may help you in the actual interview. This is an <u>excellent</u> way to establish a foundation once you get face-to-face with them or to strike up a friendly conversation about their interests which they've made public by posting their profile online. It also shows you've done your homework – and that's a good thing.

How Many Contacts are needed

Alright, so we've talked about social networking and how important it is and how you can best use if to support your efforts to locate and land that dream job. But how much time should you be spending on these sites daily? Let's face it, they can become time-consuming so you've got to have some sort of barometer about how many connections you should be establishing each day. And, by the way, you should be constantly asking for more connections on these sites.

Here are our recommendations ...

On LinkedIn®, you should make a minimum of 5-10 connections per day.

On Facebook, you should be adding a minimum of 5-10 friends per day.

And on Twitter, you should add a minimum of 10-20 connections daily. This includes people that you choose to follow as well as people who elect to follow you.

Think about that ... you can be making connections with anywhere from 20 to 40 people each day. Extrapolate that over a seven-day period and you've turned over anywhere from 140-280 stones. Are you getting' the picture how social networking can assist you in that dream-job-search?

Making connections is critical but, of these new contacts, how many do you take to the next level? Well, ultimately, that's up to you. Carefully review the new contacts you establish each day and be sure that at least two of these contacts are taken to the next level. Specifically, send them an email or, better yet, pick up the phone and chat with them live. You never know where the conversation may lead you. Hey ... today could be your lucky day!

Are You Ready for Commandment 7?

Congratulations, you're almost ready to move on to Commandment 7. But before you do, let's do a quick recap of social networking and how you can put the various sites to work for you ...

You now understand the importance of social networking in your job search

Growing your networking circle everyday and every week is critically important. You should have a goal of at least one valued new contact everyday.

Identifying target company contacts is easy but the real challenge is knowing how to correctly network with them and doing it often.

Always be willing to offer value to all people you network with and always be willing to be the giver and "Pay it Forward" because givers gain. Try it and you'll quickly see how true this is.

Finally, don't forget to visit the resources link on each social networking website for additional services available.

On to Commandment 7 … and good luck!

COMMANDMENT SEVEN

Thou Shalt Be Prepared For The Path Ahead

"Always be prepared to give an answer to everyone who asks you to give the reason for the hope that you have. But do this with gentleness and respect."

I Peter 3:15

Your 30-Second "Elevator Pitch"

Let's begin with your 30-second "elevator pitch" and how to deliver it.

If you're not familiar with this term, basically, it's being able to effectively deliver your own personal "sales pitch" in the 30 seconds you might share with another person on an elevator who's interested in you and what you're seeking. Write it, time it, and rehearse it. And after you're done rehearsing it, rehearse it a few more times! This is your chance to shine during a quick point-of-contact.

What makes for a solid "elevator pitch"?

First of all, you should speak clearly and confidently when you state your name and the industry or profession of interest, along with the specific position you're seeking. Example: "Hi, I am Dave and I am interested in finance and accounting. My interests are in brining my finance degree and experiences to an accounting and finance position."

Next, and this is very important, you should state your unique selling proposition; and for interviewing or game day, that means, what makes you different, better and more valuable to an employer than others. In other words, your strengths. Example: "I have 2 years experience with x corp which have exposed me to different approaches. In that time I saved the company over $200,000 in audits."

Close it with a statement that concludes your interests. Example: "I am confident in my ability to have the same $200,000 impact and more with your organization."

And then end it with a closing question as you wind it up – 30 seconds goes by fast when one is talking about themselves – you need to ask the question, "Do you have any openings like this, or know of anyone who does?" Or if on an interview, the questions is "What else would you like to know?"

Then be sure to smile and thank the person after they've answered.

Use the elevator pitch with everyone you meet. When you are on an interview use this to answer one of the first questions, "Tell me a little about yourself."

So, take a few moments now and sit with pen and paper to list all of these elements then write a paragraph or two that takes no longer than 30-seconds to deliver. Try it in front of a mirror, or with a friend or with a family member. Then rehearse it until it is part of you.

Feature-Benefit Presentation

Now that you have your elevator pitch perfected, its time for Features and Benefits.

Basically, this is a two-part question that you ask yourself and answer honestly as it relates to the job you're seeking, your targeted company, the hiring manager, and the business impact you can provide.

Features are skills or accomplishments and Benefits are what is the benefit to the company, hiring manager or impact on business if you are hired by the company.

This is another one of those important pad & paper exercises. The questions may seem simple but you may find yourself needing to really reflect before you answer.

So, let's begin …

- What 5 <u>features</u> (or skills) do you bring to the <u>job</u> or organization and how will they <u>benefit</u> the company?

- Example: "In my past position I cut costs by 5% which equated to $80,000. And as a results I believe I have the ability to be aware of cost cutting measures for your company as well.

- What <u>features</u> do you bring to the <u>hiring manager</u> and how will they <u>benefit</u> him or her? Remember the features should make the hiring manager's job easier.

- Example: In my previous position I completed the 6 month training program in 3 months which shows that I am a fast learner. So my ability to hit the ground running takes pressure away from you by being more profitable early.

On an interview we will want to have prepared at total of 5 of these Feature's and Benefits. Or as we call them in the employment business, Sizzling Selling Points

As with the elevator pitch, we have to do the same with the 5 Feature Benefits. We have to know them.

Know Your Interviewer

It's time to turn your attention to the person who will be conducting the first interviews.

Do some research and identify his or her interests. Next, review the interviewer's career track. See where they've worked and in what capacities. And finally, research and review the hiring manager's online profile so you better understand who he or she is and what makes them tick before the interview has even begun.

But what is important is to use this information as common denominators in your interview. For example: If you found that the interviewers hobby is canoeing, buy a magazine on canoeing and find a way to bring it up in the interview. It could be as simple as placing the magazine on top of your resume and letting him see it as you remove your resume. Trust me, he or she will ask you about it.

Remember that it is all about them and common denominators help to make it about them. Its simple human behavior. Why are your friends, friends? Because you have a lot of common denominators or things you like in common. If you didn't have common denominators they would be strangers. Make sure this employer is not a stranger.

Trust me, this will be time well-spent.

Five Frequently Asked Questions

Okay, When preparing for that first interview, you should download your own personal APP. No, not that kind of app -- but spelled the same way, APP.

APP is simply an acronym for Anticipate, Practice and Passion. Keep these three components in mind as you ready for the interview and some of the questions you'll be fielding.

Anticipating, practicing and delivering with a passion questions asked of you will make a compelling case to the hiring manager why they should invite you back for a second interview and a closer look.

Here are the top-5 most frequently asked prompts or questions asked in first interviews:

No. 1 ... "Tell me about yourself." – Be careful of this one because it's a broad-based, wide-open prompt. You must be sure you don't ramble on. This is where your 30-second elevator pitch gets used.

No. 2 -- "What are your strengths?" – Wow, this one will be . You already know your 5 feature benefits from previously in this step. This is an open invitation for you to brag a bit (and appropriately so). This is no time to be overly modest but be careful you answer the question factually and not in an overly boastful fashion.

No. 3 -- "What are your weaknesses?" – This is another one to be careful with. Nobody's perfect but don't shine the spotlight on a skill gap or it may kick you out of consideration. Instead of saying, "I'm really weak at budgeting", say "I'm continuing to hone my budgeting skills. As a matter of fact, I just signed up for a budgeting seminar" See what I mean by "couching" your answers? We all have weaknesses but when we show that we have taken steps to improve them an employer will be impressed.

No. 4 -- "Why do you want to work here?" – If there is no passion here there will be no offer. Hint: how does the companies mission statement align with your career goals. Use it.

Finally, No.5 …

"Why should I hire you?" – Again, a brief bragging opportunity for you. Look the interviewer directly in the eye and confidently and sincerely state what makes you different, better and more valuable than other candidates. Remember your 5 feature benefits.

And since we are having so much fun here is a bonus.

"What are your salary expectations?"

Try your best to not give a direct amount. It is like negotiating in a sale, the first person who gives an amount loses.

Answer instead, "Money is important to me as I have bills and responsibilities as everyone else. But, what is most important to me is the opportunity in the company."

Now ask the interviewer, "What range do you feel is fair?"

Anticipate ... Practice ... Passion. Time to download your APP!

Top 5 Questions to Ask in an Interview

Now its time to play stump the interviewer and ask questions like a game show.

Just kidding.

But it is time to ask questions that show the interviewer that you are focused, prepared and committed.

An interview should be like a two-way street where questions and answers flow back and forth between interviewer and interviewee. You'll know when it's appropriate for you to ask questions -- or your interviewer may ask if you have any questions for him or her.

So, be prepared. You must have questions.

Here are 5 questions you should ask in your initial interview that will help you to decide if this opportunity is for you as well as impress the interviewer. Wow, that's a two for one.

No. 1 – "What can I do to make your job easier?"

Asking this questions goes a long way in sharing with the employer that you are making his decision a smart one. Why do employers hire? To make their jobs easier.

No. 2 – "What would you expect me to accomplish in my first three months on the job that would validate your decision to hire me?"

Listen and then repeat what they said. Example: "That's terrific. You have just described my abilities to a tee."

No. 3 – "If I give a 110% and are one of your best employees, where can I be with your company in three to five years?"

This shows that you are thinking long term and are willing to do what it takes to be successful.

No. 4 – "What do you like most about working here?" This question gives you an opportunity to gain more common denominators and insight on the company.

And, No.5 …

"What will be the biggest challenge in this position?" Listen and then give one or two solutions.

Be sure to write these questions down and have them easily accessible so when your chance to switch from interviewee to interviewer presents itself, you'll be ready. Trust me, the hiring manager will be impressed.

Now that we know what questions to ask in an interview, maybe we should take a look at what not to ask.

Top 5 Questions NOT to Ask in an Interview

Now, let's turn the coin over and focus on the Top-5 Questions **NOT** to Ask in an Interview.

Preparing for and managing the interview is as much about putting your best foot forward as it is about making sure you don't shoot yourself in that foot. Here are the five questions you don't even want to think about asking your hiring manager in a first interview:

No. 1 – "How much are you going to pay me?"

Asking this questions show you are only interested in the economics today versus the opportunity of the position.

No. 2 – "When can I start taking vacation days?"

No. 3 – "Do I have to get dressed up all of the time?"

No. 4 – "Can I work flex time?"

Numbers Two, three and Four, the appropriate place for these question is after an offer has been made. So, lets focus on getting an offer first.

And, No. 5 ...

"You don't do drug testing or background checks do you?"

Obviously we are joking here. But the bottom line is if you have to ask this question, you will need to be honest with the employer as to why you are asking this. Better to bring it out here that to have them find it out later. Honesty carries a lot of weight.

There are deal-<u>makers</u> and deal-<u>breakers</u>. Each one of these are deal-<u>breakers</u> so steer away from these questions in any form during the first interview. Remember, your goal is to get an offer. At this point in the hiring process,, it's all about <u>them</u>, not you.

Positive Spin on Negative Past

Let's talk about how you handle what can be a very delicate and awkward situation in an interview setting – putting a positive spin on a negative past, <u>your</u> past. Maybe your past.

Hey, let's face it, everybody has a blemish or two on their record because we're all human. The key is to find the best way to address the issue without hurting your chances of being hired by the interested employer.

First rule of thumb … never lie … ever … <u>ever</u>! (Did I say "ever". You bet I did.)

In today's information age, it's simply too easy for an employer to check your background and to learn more about you than you may want them to know. And beyond that, it's simply not ethical and that's not the way you want to begin a potential long-term relationship with a company you truly desire to work for.

We recommend a pre-emptive strike; that is, find a way for <u>you</u> to cover the issue or experience <u>before</u> the interviewer discovers it. This keeps you out of a defensive posture if you were to be questioned about it -- and a defensive posture will <u>always</u> do damage to your chances of being hired.

When summarizing the negative issue or experience, take the high road. Don't be negative. Don't blame. Don't point fingers at anyone. Specifically, don't trash previous employers or your former manager.

Accept responsibility for your part of the issue or experience and share what you learned from it. And be positive and passionate about your learning's. For instance, if a project ran over budget, you could say, "What I realized from this experience is that it's critically important to monitor the budget on a daily basis and get a fact-based list of actual expenses incurred to-date." This demonstrates professional growth.

Finally, you can further neutralize any potential whiplash effect of a negative issue or experience from your past by providing references and contact information for 2-3 former bosses or peers who can attest to your work ethic and character.

Hey, if fate hands you a lemon, you make lemonade, right?

Are You Ready for Commandment 8

We're just about done with Commandment 7 – and you're doing great!

But before we move on to Commandment 8, let's quickly summarize what we just covered. Here we go …

You now know the importance of writing and rehearsing your elevator pitch. Live It! Love It! Breathe It!

You understand you must download your personal "APP" before you enter the first interview. A-P-P … <u>Anticipate</u>, <u>Practice</u> and have a <u>Passion</u> when delivering your 5 Features and Benefits.

You've conducted your research and have common denominators about your interviewer which allows you to establish a strong rapport in the first interview and <u>increases</u> your chances of being brought back for Round 2.

You've prepared and rehearsed your answers to the 5 Frequently Asked Questions.

You've prepared and rehearsed your Top-5 Questions to Ask the Interviewer. You also know what questions NOT to ask and why in the first interview.

And, finally ...

You understand, at this point of the hiring process, it's all about their needs, not yours and that the goal of an interview is to get an offer.

I believe you're ready to move on to Commandment 8. Congratulations and keep up the awesome work!

COMMANDMENT EIGHT

Thou Shalt Interview To Get The Job Offer

"Commit to the Lord whatever you do, and your plans will succeed."
Prov. 16:3

Applicant Be Aware

It is time for your interview. So, let's get started …

Before the actual interview, be sure to double-check the accuracy of any information that has been provided the employer on a formal application, in emails, correspondence, phone conversations, notes, etc.

Specifically, I'm talking about employment dates, positions or job titles, prior salary, and stated reasons for leaving. Make sure there's no ambiguity or incorrect information that's been accidentally communicated. If we discover an inaccuracy, be prepared to pro-actively address it in the interview so we don't raise any suspicions of having been less than truthful. That would likely be a deal-breaker for you.

Gather all of this fundamental information and memorize it so, if you need to reference it during the interview, you'll be speaking accurately.

Purpose of the Interview

Before we get into the specifics of how to manage the actual face-to-face interview, you must understand that the purpose of the interview is to convince the interviewer that you:

- Can do the job
- Are the right person for the job
- Will make the manager's job easier
- Are passionate about the job, and finally …
- You generate the perception that you want the job and the company

The key to these five bullets is in the clarity and sincerity of your answers.

How you present your feature benefits, which should include specific examples of how you 've created solutions or solved challenges in the past.

Of course, never forget the three P's: Professional appearance, Personality and Passion.

That's a lot to accomplish, but hey, its Show Time!

Rapport Building In The Interview

Perhaps the most important intangible element in a face-to-face interview is the rapport you're able to establish with the individuals conducting the interview. In fact, building a strong rapport in the interview is a critical step in the process of landing that offer. It is absolutely true that people like to work and associate with other people with which they have chemistry.

So, how do you establish a strong rapport?

Begin with the initial, face-to-face greeting which means a genuine, warm smile, direct eye contact and a firm, professional handshake.

Look around the room and notice something on the desk, walls, etc. that is personal to the interviewer and can be talked about. An example might be awards or plaques displayed on shelves or on the wall.
This is called Common denominators.

Other ways to create common denominators is make a connection with appropriate conversation starters like the weather (be positive, don't moan about how gloomy it is) and seasonal topics like holidays such as asking "Do you have big plans for the Fourth of

July?" These not only help you to break the ice but are good to use in Thank you notes.

In all cases, keep it positive and upbeat which will show you focus on the positive, not the negative.

You will establish a strong rapport by creating chemistry and a desire to collaborate on topics of discussion, or to find other common denominators that foster friendly, positive interaction which makes you more desirable to be around. This will be accomplished by exuding energy and enthusiasm in your comments, finding opportunities to point out how <u>you</u> can help <u>them</u>, and by asking "How can I make <u>your</u> job easier?"

This all adds up to a "feel good" atmosphere and you're the catalyst. In tandem with your stellar resume' and complete understanding that, at this stage, it's all about the employer, you can't <u>help</u> but make a positive impression.

Finally, make your passion for the job obvious and sincere.

Interview Preparation

Now it's time to <u>really</u> roll up your sleeves and prepare for the interview. Time for a little research. It is good to research the company online, in the media, and by speaking with friends, family and contacts who may have a perspective or insight that can help. And, don't forget to research the interviewer and learn all you can about them.

You'll be amazed at how much you can learn about someone before ever meeting them face-to-face. If you know somebody who has dealt with your interviewer, speak to them and ask them for the best way to approach and connect with this person. Make notes about them and use these as the common denominators we discussed in our previous video.

Next, its time to read the job description – not once, not twice, but three times, or more. Read it until each of the details can be committed to memory. Find ways to connect the points you're making in your interview with the <u>specific</u> requirements and responsibilities of the position you desire. In other words, using our Feature Benefits presentations to be specific to this job description and requirements. The more you're able to establish a "fit" between our skills and experience with the job requirements, the more likely it is you will be given stronger consideration and, ultimately, get an offer.

Finally, think back to previous jobs and experience and jot down different structured behavioral examples; situations where you addressed a challenge and came up with a meaningful solution. When possible, provide specific, fact-based evidence of how your leadership and decisions helped address a situation or solved a problem.

Structured behavioral examples are powerful components of a successful interview.

Prepping For a Structured Behavioral Interview

Prepping for a Structured Behavioral Interview. So what does that mean? Well, let's take a look.

Once you know the job requirements in the job posting its time to sit down with pad & pen – or at your laptop or PC – and begin to list past projects, jobs and other potentially relevant experiences. Think back to specific examples of things you developed or created or executed that were impressive and would connect with specific requirements listed in the job posting.

Don't overestimate the importance of things that you might think are insignificant because they may have been very significant to your peers, colleagues or your employer.

After listing these examples, anticipate probing questions the interviewer might ask about each example and think carefully about how best to answer their questions. A good place to start is what journalism professors call "the five Ws and H" – that is, Who, What, Where, When, Why and How? Answer each of these questions succinctly and factually for each example.

Another thing …

When asked a question by your interviewer, resist the urge to blurt out an immediate response – which often happens when your level of nervousness is elevated. It's perfectly fine – and, in fact, often impressive – if you pause to reflect and carefully consider your answer before speaking. If you find yourself overly nervous, it is okay to share this with the interviewer…..It shows YOU CARE.

However, be prepared to articulate your answer no more than 7 seconds after the question has been asked or you may risk coming across as having fabricated an answer – and we don't want that! So, it's OK to briefly pause and reflect before speaking.

And by all means, if you don't clearly understand the question, be sure to say something like, "I'm not sure I fully understand the question and I am aware of the importance of accurate communication in business. Could you please ask that again?" The interviewer will most likely be happy to rephrase the question and maybe conclude that you are an accurate and effective communicator.....Hey, at this stage, you are!

Sample Behavioral Interview Questions

Okay, let's take an even closer look at "structured behavior" interviews through some of the questions you'll likely be asked.

First of all, remember the acronym SBO. "S" stands for Situation, "B" for Behaviors you used to make the situation happen and "O" stands for Outcome or results of your behaviors. Thinking in terms of Situation, Behavior and Outcome will help you effectively "frame" your answers to Behavior Interview –style questions.

Anticipate that the interviewer is going to ask questions similar to these:

"Give me an example of being creative in solving a problem."

Now, this where you go back to prior experiences or jobs to provide an examples. Past experience predicts future performance. Behavioral examples show the interviewer how you have done something in the past and this predicts how you will do it, if they hire you to do it for their company.

An example of an answer to the question:

"There was a time in my last job, with XYZ Corporation, where we had to bring a new product to market. We realized that we weren't sure whether it addressed our target market's needs and we didn't know what those needs were."

Now, the interviewer is going to ask you probes to find out what "Behaviors" you used to solve this problem.

A question he/she may ask is: "What steps did you take to solve the problem?"

A good behavioral answer could be: "I created a 10 step survey that was emailed out to our prospective clients to find out exactly what they needed?"

The lasting probing question the interviewer will most probably ask is : "What was the end result?"

And a good answer would be; "The survey results gave us the information we needed, to customize the product to fulfill the exact needs of our customers."

The interviewer is also likely to ask a question that will require you to think of a time you were NOT able to do something. This is called "Balance seeking" information and gives the interviewer a chance to see how you have handled situations that have not gone smoothly. This is a much needed skill now.

A sample question: "Describe a situation where you were NOT able to resolve a conflict at work?"

The answer: "There was a time I worked with a very challenging colleague and we were not seeing eye to eye on how to resolve customer complaints. She was actually disrespectful to me in our departmental staff meeting. I tried speaking to her privately, but nothing changed"

The interviewer may then ask: "What did you do to resolve this?"

Your answer might be: "I asked my manager to mediate a meeting between us."
The interviewer then may ask:" How did it all turn out?"

Your answer can be "We were not able to resolve our differences and I decided that I wanted to stay with the company, so I transferred to another department and was able to continue my loyalty to the company until the headquarters transferred to another state."
These are examples of very standard behavioral interview questions that are important for the interviewer as he or she

assesses whether or not you're a viable candidate. At the same time, they're also gift-wrapped, golden invitations to you to <u>showcase</u> yourself and to <u>highlight</u> some of your <u>previous</u> successes.

So, remember S, B, O. Situation, Behavior, Outcome. Frame your answers to interview questions and prompts in this style and you'll likely find yourself moving on to the next step in your search for that great job.

The Telephone Interview (your setting)

Let's talk about phone interviews and your setting and environment when that big call comes in. Where should you take the call and how should you handle it? Here's the scoop.

Most likely we will know a precise date and time when the phone interview is going to take place so plan your day such that you will be in a quiet place at the scheduled time – no background music, no barking dogs, no running water or dishwashers, no noisy children – or noisy adults for that matter!

Interruptions, distractions, we don't want any of that. So, by all means, ignore the call-waiting feature on your phone should a second call come in while the interview is being conducted. I know I know, that's obvious. Just a healthy reminder because most employers hate that distraction.

When taking the call, we want to use our professional voice and speak clearly and eloquently and stay away from slang language. It's critical that you come across as completely polished and articulate versus hey dude and what's up.

Many people find they are able to speak more professionally and in a more polished fashion when they stand vs. sitting in a chair or lounging on a couch. Your body posture has a lot to do with inflection and tone so you may want to take the call and answer your interview questions while standing. One thing though … the biggest intangible on every interview is energy and passion. With the phone interview, the interviewer only has the sound of your voice to judge your personality versus your physical presence in a face 2 face interview. So, lots of energy.

Next, be sure to have a pad and pen handy when the call comes in because you'll like need to take notes. And don't be uncomfortable asking the interviewer for an extra moment or two when you're jotting down notes. You can say, "May I take a moment to write that down?" Your interviewer will appreciate the fact that you care enough to document key information exchanged in the phone interview.

If you want to make the phone interview easier, keep previous notes and resume handy to quickly refer to them and refresh your memory when necessary. Actually, this is one of the secret advantages of a phone interview because the person on the other end of the line will likely assume you're delivering the answers spontaneously when, in fact, you may be referring to some of your research notes. It's almost like taking an open-book test, so capitalize on this benefit.

Finally, and perhaps most importantly, the goal of the phone interview is to get the interviewer to say yes to a face 2 face interview, Now. So by far the best way to end the phone interview is to say, "Do you have any additional questions for me? Thank you for your time and I am very interested in pursuing this further. What are the next steps and when you do you want me there?"

<u>Filling Out Application</u>

The application can be so basic yet so many conclusions can be drawn by
interviewers from the application.

For example: Is the applicant organized? Are they focused? Do they care? It is one of the first impressions that we will make.

So let's begin filling out the application.

Application 101 suggests spelling, grammar and neatness are easy disqualifiers for an interviewer. Salary desired? Guess what, we do not want to put a figure here. Know why? Because it is like negotiating in a sale, the first person who gives an amount loses. If you give a figure, you could wind up either being too high or too low. If you are too high, you can knock yourself out of contention over what winds up being a couple of dollars a week. And if you are too low, you can wind up taking a pay cut before you even start. So the best answer is open.

Sometimes an application is used as a test. If you leave areas blank or put down, "See resume" this implies to a company that you might take short cuts or not follow directions on the job. So, it's in our best interest to fill it out completely.

Which leads us to "reasons for leaving" we share in the Face 2 Face Interview, these should be more about going towards enhancing our career rather than moving away from a problem or an issue.

That's the application. We don't want to overcomplicate it. However realize, this is a representation of us and your first impression.

The Face to Face or In-Person Interview

Hey, congratulations! You <u>aced</u> the phone interview and you've gotten to the next step, the face-to-face interview. Let's take a look at how to handle <u>this</u> one.

There are three phases to a face to face interview. They are the introduction, the body and the all important closing of the interview.

Lets begin with phase one, the introduction.

First, dress professionally. Unless the interviewer specifically says to dress a specific way for the interview, always dress in a suit. You never get a second chance to make a great first impression. So, shine those shoes, hide the piercings, cut the hair and minimal makeup.

Shifting gears …

Prior to the interview, get driving directions to the interview location whether it's their offices or at a coffee shop – which <u>often</u> happens today. Prior to the interview, you may even want to actually <u>drive</u> the route at the same time you would be driving to the actual interview. This way, you'll know how much time to allow and you'll lessen your chances of getting lost en route on the big day. Take special note to the time of the day for the interview as traffic patterns vary,

Of special importance is to arrive 15 -20 minutes early for the interview. In most cases, an application will be filled out prior to your actual face 2 face interview. Many forget to calculate this into their arrival time. One of the bigger Interviewer pet peeves is an interview that begins 20 minutes after the interview time because they had to wait for you to fill out the application. Additionally, arriving early allows you to relax and not be rushed.

Let take a moment on the resume. It is always good to have multiple, hard copies of your resume' on-hand. In fact, it is wise to bring along more copies than actually needed just in case the opportunity arises to meet several <u>other</u> people while at the employer's office. Let's also not forget our personal business cards.

When you arrive for the face-to-face interview and are greeted, extend a <u>firm</u> handshake while looking the person directly in the eye. This eye contact should continue throughout the entire interview.

And remember to look around the room and gather your common denominators as it is about the right time to use them.

So that is the Introduction phase of the interview. Fairly basic but important as we all know nothing beats a great first impression.

Second phase is the Body of the Interview. This is where most of the conversation takes place.

We have already done the research and have our list of specific behavioral examples that directly relate to the requirements stated in the job description. Along with the behavioral examples we also have our top 5 questions to ask the interviewer. This is an excellent way to demonstrate to the interviewer that we are prepared, organized and focused on their opportunity.

One of the first questions an interviewer asks is, "Tell me a little about yourself?" This is the ultimate place to use your interview version of the 30-second elevator pitch.

Normally, the interviewer will proceed to examine your skills sets as they relate to the job description. Remember those Features and Benefits? Bingo, here is where they fit.

Work history and reasons for leaving are now right around the corner. Know and discuss your **specific** dates of employment, your achievements and accomplishment and relate them to the job description. Be able to explain any gaps in work history.

When discussing Reasons for Leaving previous jobs, we want them to be good ones. Let's share a few examples. Leaving for advancement, more personal growth, and the company downsized are just a few. Try to phrase your reasons for leaving to be more about going towards enhancing our career rather than moving away from a problem or an issue.

Examples of going away from a problem or issue: I hated my boss. I didn't get the raise I thought I should have. Its too many hours or days t work. Etc.

Somewhere in the interview, it will become our turn to ask questions. Okay, whoop out your top 5 questions and please, please don't include the questions you know not to ask.

Now let's spend a moment on money. When the issue of money comes up it is normally best to let the employer address the subject first. This usually happens with "What are your salary expectations?"

Try your best to not give a direct amount. It is like negotiating in a sale, the first person who gives an amount loses.

Answer instead, "Money is important to me as I have bills and responsibilities as everyone else. But, what is most important to me is the opportunity in the company."

As we stated previously about handling any major blemishes, if you have any being proactive is the way to go. Honesty is the best policy and they will most likely find it sooner or later. By us addressing the blemish, the employer may look at the information as an observation as apposed to them discovering it on their own which usually creates a hesitation. So, as previously discussed, be honest, accept responsibility and be positive.

Always remember to be enthused, listen intently and exude positive energy...

We are now prepared for the face to face interview.......Well, almost. We are missing one key element...

Closing Out The Interview

Closing the interview…. Yes it certainly is a Big key element!

Let's take a closer look.

Once you sense the interviewer is ready to wrap up, be sure to ask them, "Are there any other questions you have for me?" If not, close with a power statement like "Mr. Jones, there's <u>nobody</u> who will harder for you than <u>me</u>. If you give me a chance, I will not let you down."

You should also open the door to the next step by asking for the next interview or, if this <u>is</u> the final round, asking for the actual job. You can accomplish this by asking, "So, what are the next steps and when would you like for me to be available?"

Or, if this is the <u>final</u> round of interviews prior to an offer being formally extended, come right out and enthusiastically ask, "When do I start?" This will provide the interviewer the opportunity to give you the answer you're for looking for or, at the very least, will demonstrate your confidence and sincere desire to be the candidate selected for the job. You may feel it's a bit bold but we are here to MAKE IT HAPPEN NOW…. not hope that it may happen... This is the most important question one can make on an interview, period.

The most successful sales professionals in the world are the ones who are unafraid to ask for the business. And today, you're a sales professional and the product and service you're selling is <u>you</u>. So, let's close the deal!

Finally, another firm handshake with direct eye contact. Thank the interviewer by name – "I truly appreciate your time today, Ms. Smith and I look forward to hearing from you." With that, stand tall and walk confidently away. Don't linger and stay any longer than is appropriate.

Are You Ready for Commandment 9

Alright, we've covered a lot of ground here in Commandment 8. Congratulations. Because when you implement the systems in Commandment 8, you will find yourself going to Commandment 9 more often.

But, first, let's do a quick review …

We will be feeling fine for step nine when:

We have convinced the interviewer that we are the right person for the job and have brought out our 3 P's … Personal Appearance, Passion and Personality

We have learned to develop rapport and chemistry through common denominators.

We have adopted a behavioral interview style and remember **SBO.**

We are confident, prepared and can demonstrate energy and passion in a phone interview

We understand the application represents us and is our first impression and we are confident and can readily implement the three phases of the interview which are the Introduction, The Body and Closing the Interview.

And lastly, Enthusiastically **Ask the question** the number one question, "When do I start?"

Got that? Well done! I believe you're ready to move forward!

COMMANDMENT

NINE

Thou Shalt Follow Up For Success

"I have fought the good fight, I have finished the race,
I have kept the faith."
2 Timothy 4:7

The Keys to Interview Follow-Up

Welcome to Follow-Up. You have accomplished and learned so much. There is light at the end of the employment tunnel, isn't there?

But a word of caution, until you have a formal offer, which we will cover in step 10, now is not the time to stop what got you here. So, it is crucial that you are still proactive in generating first interviews.

So you know you've "aced" the interview, you've got a pep in your step, and you can't wait to get home and share with others the good news that things are looking more and more promising each day. So what do you do with all the energy and excitement?

Well, the first thing you need to do is sit down and write a thank-you note and a thank you email to each person you interviewed with ... and to stay ahead of your competition, you will want to do it within 24 hours; the sooner, the better.

What should the "Thank You" note say? Check out the third video in this step and you will have your answer.

While we live in an era of technology and immediate communication, don't ever take for granted the personal and powerful gesture of a hand-written follow-up note. This doesn't have to be any more than 3-4 sentences long because it's more about the gesture – you taking the time to do this -- than it is about the information contained in the note card.

After sending a follow-up email, you should make a phone call to the hiring manager to thank them for the interview within 24 hours of sending it.

How do you do an award winning "Thank You" call? You guessed it, watch the next video in this step.

Finally … remember, follow-up "thank you" notes and/or emails aren't merely a consideration, they are an absolute must.

Making a Thank-You Call

You've sent your Thank you note and email and you've got the hiring manager on the other end of the phone. There are some things you should say and there are definitely some things you shouldn't say.

Let's first look at the things you should say ...

Begin with, *"I appreciate all the departmental and company information you provided me. It helped me gain an even better understanding of the opportunity."*

It's also critical that you use this valuable point-of-contact to reiterate why you believe your skills are a match for the position, and to re-state very sincerely your excitement about the opportunity as well as your passion for the responsibilities you would have in this particular job.

Finally, end the call by saying passionately, *"I am excited about the*

prospect of joining your company and I give you my word that no one will

work harder for you than me to show that you made the right decision to

hire me."

"I look forward to hearing from you once you've made your decision. When would you suggest that I follow up?"

So, that's what you <u>should</u> say. It shows the three C's. Conviction, which generated the impression and eliminates the question that you want to work for them. Confidence, in your abilities to do the job. And Conscientious, that you have great work ethic.

Now, let's look at a few no-no's … things you must avoid saying when speaking with the hiring manager in your follow-up phone call.

It may seem obvious but you wouldn't believe how many people will ask when vacation kicks in. Uh-uh. Save that one for after you've been hired and have been in the organization for a little while.

Another question you should avoid is, "How much will I make when I start?" That's a discussion for later in the hiring process. And avoid being apologetic because you'll simply call attention to your weaknesses. Don't say, "I'm not sure I meet <u>all</u> of your needs, but I meet most of them." Another no-no.

Finally, don't ever say anything along the lines of, "The job isn't <u>exactly</u> what I was looking for, but I want to give it a try." This will only spotlight your lack of excitement and passion for the opportunity.

This is pretty obvious stuff but it's still a healthy reminder.

The Thank You Note or EMail

Let's take a closer look at the follow-up thank-you note and email you're getting ready to write. First of all, it should never be more than four paragraphs with the first paragraph used to state your appreciation. Example: "(Employers Name), I wanted to thank you for taking the time in your busy day to talk with me yesterday."

The second paragraph should thank them for the information they shared with you in the interview. Example: "It was very impressive to learn about the growth plans your company has and the passion you have about its growth."

The third paragraph should cite some examples and should also reference how your skills match the requirements outlined in the job description. Example: "I am confident that my experience, work ethic and desire are an outstanding match not only for the position but for your company as well."

Finally, you closing paragraph should express your excitement about working for the company because it's an opportunity for you to put your passion to work. Example: "The prospect of joining your organization excites me and I give you my word that no one will work harder for you to show that you made an appropriate decision. I look forward to exceeding your expectations."

Now, that shouldn't take too long. And you never know, it just might send you to the top of the list of candidates.

The Second Interview

Well, there's good news and some not-so-good news …

The good news is you've been contacted for a second interview which could be face-to-face or an interview conducted over the phone or by teleconference.

The not-so-good news is that a second interview only means you've made it to the next step. Congratulations … but don't assume you have the job.

This is no time to ease up or become complacent or overly confident. You must treat the second interview as if it were your first interview with the company. You took that one very seriously and you must do the same with this one – though your preparation will be a little different in Round II. It will be more <u>job</u>-specific. We'll get into more detail in the following video.

Prepping For the Second and Subsequent Interviews

Alright, you're making progress. You've secured that second interview and now it's time to prepare.

The first thing you should do is begin to identify additional behavioral examples that you didn't cover in the initial interview.

The next thing you should do is review any and all company information you've acquired to the point that it's top-of-mind for you. You should also research the company's competition thoroughly so you have an awareness of the competitive challenges.

Another important prep step is to do some additional research on the hiring manager and use this info as common denominators as you continue to establish a positive rapport with them. Remember what you learned about using Social Networking to obtain information about interviewers? Well it is back in Step 6 video 5 if you need a refresher.

Finally, prepare your questions for the interviewer with the final question being something like, "I really want to work for you. When can I start?" I'm serious. Do not be afraid to say it this way. It shows confidence, you have made your decision and you are being proactive by making it happen versus letting it happen. And that is what got you this far.

What are you waiting for? You've got work to do!

<u>Post-Interview Follow Up</u>

This is may sound a bit repetitive but you know how hard you have worked to get this far and it is not the time to take shortcuts. I like to think of it as <u>reiterating</u> very important follow-up once you've gone through your interview; in this case, the second interview.

Send a thank-you note and a thank you email to each person you interviewed with … and to stay ahead of your competition, you will want to do it within 24 hours; the sooner, the better.

You should already know what the "Thank You" note say? If you do not remember, Check out the third video in this step and you will have your answer.

After sending a follow-up email, you should make a phone call to the hiring manager to thank them for the interview within 24 hours of sending it.

Once you have the hiring manager live on the phone, re-state, "I truly enjoyed speaking with you and I appreciate you sharing your time and insights about this opportunity and the company and that I want to work for your organization"

Finally, and most importantly, follow-up "thank you's" are not merely a consideration, they are a must!

Are You Ready for Commandment 10

Wow, you're moving things along quite nicely. Congratulations. You're just about ready to move on to Commandment 10. But first, let's recap Commandment 9.

You now understand the importance of sending a thank-you email immediately after an interview. And you know to follow up on this email within 24 hours of sending it.

We also know you must send a handwritten note card within 24 hours – if not sooner – and then follow up with a phone call immediately.

You know that a second interview is a good sign but it doesn't mean you have the job. Treat it as if it were your _first_ interview with the company.

As you prepare for the second interview, you're going to identify additional behavioral examples that you didn't cover in the initial interview. And you must also continue to research the company, the company's competition, and the industry.

Finally, you're going to prepare _your_ questions for the Hiring Manager and close with the question, "I really want to work for you. When can I start?"

So, that's it. WOW! You're ready for Step 10. Go get 'em!

COMMANDMENT TEN

Thou Shalt Get a Job Offer

"Hope deferred makes the heart sick, but a longing fulfilled is a tree of life."

Prov. 13:12

What is a Job Offer?

We are proud of you. Now we have an offer…..Well not so fast. We probably got here by not taking short cuts. And now is definitely not the time to start taking them.

This may sound a little odd but how do you know when you've actually received a job offer? Some conversations may sound like an offer has been extended but an offer's not an offer without the following three items …

First, an offer includes a specific salary. (If you're pursuing a straight commission sales position, it should include information about the training and support available to you from the company and any benefits you will be eligible for.) A salaried offer should include a specific amount whether hourly, weekly or yearly, how it is paid, how many hours it is based upon and whether it includes overtime.

Secondly, a formal job offer will include a specific starting date; not ""in two weeks" or "next month" but an exact date. In the absence of this, you may need to ask the hiring manager, "What is the specific date you need for me to start?"

Sometimes an employer will say they are not sure whether it will be in 2 or 3 weeks. A good way to overcome this is to ask "What is the farthest out worst case scenario of a start date."

If he says, Three weeks. Then select a specific day you can both agree on. This may seem insignificant, but many times employers have reneged on an offer by saying a specific date was never agreed upon. How disappointing that would be after all of this hard work.

Thirdly, an actual job offer will include your specific work location or where you would begin training.

One final note. If at all possible, get your offer in writing. It is called an offer letter.

What if something about the offer is not what you expected?

Don't Say 'No' Immediately To a Job Offer You Do Not Like

Alright, we have an actual job offer...but it's not exactly what we were hoping for. It might be a salary issue, work schedule, start date, anything.

The first thing we should do is politely ask the hiring manager if you can get back with them in 1-2 days and also share with them why. Something to the effect of: "Thanks so much for the offer. Is it okay if I follow up with you within 2 days because the X could be a little more of a challenge than I anticipated and I want to find a way to make it work because that aside, I really want to work for you." This gives them a sense of your concerns and they just may rethink their offer.

Next, let's go back and review the CLAMPS notes ... how we ranked and rated Challenge, Lifestyle, Advancement, Money, Prestige and Stability. This will serve as a memory refresher to reestablished your priority considerations, and why.

Finally, when considering your options take a _logical_ approach vs. an emotional approach. How close is the offer to what we were seeking? This is no time to get hung up on pride issues. We don't want to pass up on our dream job because of a short term challenge.

For instance, let's say the annual salary is $2,000 less than what you were seeking. Let's break that down ...

Two-thousand dollars divided by 52 weeks is approximately $40 per week. Factor in taxes and you're only missing out on about $28 a week. Divide that $28 by seven days and the difference is only $4 a day. The question that begs asking is, do we really want to walk away from this opportunity for $4 per day?

Now ... how much did that gourmet coffee cost you this morning at the coffee shop? Uh-huh, thought so. Be sure to make a logical, rationale decision vs. an emotional decision that you might regret later.

How Do I Enhance My Job Offer

So here we are with an offer that has been extended. An additional day or two has been asked for to consider it and now we want to see if we can get them to enhance things a bit.

How do we do that? If money is the issue – and it often is – how can we get more?

Upon reconnecting with the hiring manager, be honest and share with them what is most important. This is a wonderful opportunity to restate that, "No one will work harder for you than me. You have my word on that. However, I was hoping there may be some flexibility on the starting salary?"

The hiring manager will either answer "yes" or "no" or they may need to consult with someone else and get back. If they say they are unable to increase the level of compensation, perhaps there is a possibility for more vacation time, enhanced benefits or mileage reimbursement, etc. While salary may not be negotiable, other parts of the offer may be.

Please do not let one item dictate your emotions. It is important that we share with the employer a passion on their team. This should be a conversation not a negotiation or an interrogation.

Accepting a Job Offer and Before You Start

So you've made the big decision – you've decided to accept the offer. Let's take a look at what we want to do to close the deal so we are ready for a fantastic Day 1 on the new job.

First, formally accept the offer <u>directly</u> from the employer, not a third-party if it can be avoided.

Next, politely request an offer letter be sent via FAX or overnight delivery so we have the offer in writing.

Lets thank them sincerely and reiterate that we will give them 110%.

Next, ask for the specific start date, time and location to report to work.

Now we will want to clarify the company's dress code before our start date. Don't want to be under-dressed – or over-dressed.

And in the time period between now and the start date, ask the employer how to best prepare for the first day on the job. This shows commitment and initiative and will further convince the hiring manager that he or she made a solid decision in offering you the position.

Immediately send a thank-you letter to the hiring manager and show excitement and enthusiasm by including a line like, "I look forward to exceeding your expectations".

Next, go online and get driving directions from home to the new work location then go out and actually drive the route at the same time of the day as your commute would be so you know exactly where you're going and how long it's going to take to get there.

<u>Celebrate!</u>

Finally, get together with loved ones and congratulate yourself because you … are a winner. You have been hired. Way to go!

Made in the USA
San Bernardino, CA
01 July 2016